Dear Reader,

This book came about because so many people asked for a way to help children with jitters on the first day of school—or in other moments when they feel anxious about meeting people for the first time.

Here are a few tips to help you get the most out of this book.

• **Repeat the mantra out loud with your child.** Bear and the other characters in this story use a mantra as a calming device—and kids can too. Repetition makes it effective. The mantra in this book comes from one of my most popular songs, "Everybody's Got a Heartbeat." You can listen to it here: kirawilley.com/books.

• **Use the prompts!** These reflection questions encourage children to think about and express how they're feeling. This self-awareness is a critical social-emotional skill for kids to develop. Take your time moving through the book, and if a particular prompt leads to a discussion, let it unfold naturally to see where it goes.

• **Pull this book out for any "firsts."** Kids will have lots of firsts as they grow. This book is perfect for times when butterflies arise relating to meeting new people and fitting in. It's a great reminder that our differences are part of life, and that we all have a heartbeat—a rhythm we all share!

I hope you and the children in your life find this book helpful! I'd love to hear from you. You can find me at kirawilley.com.

Kira

For all the dedicated and hardworking teachers
helping today's children grow to be mindful
and kind citizens of the world
—K.W.

For my brother, Alex,
the greatest companion on the walk to school
—A.B.

Text copyright © 2023 by Kira Willey
Cover art and interior illustrations copyright © 2023 by Anni Betts

All rights reserved. Published in the United States by Rodale Kids, an imprint of
Random House Children's Books, a division of Penguin Random House LLC, New York.

Rodale and the colophon are registered trademarks and Rodale Kids is a trademark of
Penguin Random House LLC.

Visit us on the Web! rhcbooks.com

Educators and librarians, for a variety of teaching tools, visit us at RHTeachersLibrarians.com

Library of Congress Cataloging-in-Publication Data is available upon request.
ISBN 978-0-593-48672-6 (hardcover) — ISBN 978-0-593-48673-3 (ebook)

The artist created the illustrations for this book digitally.
The text of this book is set in 15-point Intro.
Book design by Jan Gerardi

MANUFACTURED IN CHINA
10 9 8 7 6 5 4 3 2 1
First Edition

Breathe Like a Bear
First Day of School Worries

A Story with a Calming Mantra and Mindful Prompts

Kira Willey

Illustrated by Anni Betts

Rodale Kids   RODALE KiDS   New York

Bear is so excited for her very first day of school with all the other forest animals! She has eaten her breakfast and is ready to go. But she still feels a little anxious. It feels like there are butterflies in her tummy.

Do you ever feel anxious?

Bear heads off to school.
Her friend Bird swoops down.
He's going to school too.
Bear tells Bird about the
butterflies in her tummy. Bird's
a good listener. He's quiet until
Bear finishes talking.

Are you a good listener?

"I feel anxious too," Bird says. "What if someone at school doesn't like my feathers or thinks they're too colorful?"

Do you **tell your friends** how you feel?

Owl pops her head out of her hole in a tree.

"Hello," she hoots. "I have a mantra for when I am anxious. A mantra is a set of words you say that can change how you feel. You can say it out loud, or you can just think it. My mantra reminds me that we are all connected. I feel it in my heart."

"I'd like a mantra," says Bear.
"Me too!" chirps Bird.

Owl takes a long, deep breath in . . . and lets all the air out. She says:

"Breathe in, breathe out. Everybody has a heartbeat. Breathe in, breathe out. It's a rhythm we all share."

Bird and Bear take a long, deep breath in . . .
and let it all the way out. They say Owl's mantra.

"Breathe in, breathe out.
Everybody has a heartbeat.
Breathe in, breathe out.
It's a rhythm we all share."

Can you take a
deep breath in and let it out?
Can you say the mantra?

Bird looks at his brightly colored feathers,
and Bear looks at her brown fur.
"Feathers and fur may *look* very different,"
says Bear, "but they do the same job."
"They protect us and keep us warm!" chirps Bird.

What do you like to wear?

"Thank you, Owl!" they call as they go on down the path to school.
"Have a great first day," hoots Owl.

The friends come to a clearing. Bear and Bird see Fawn having a snack on his way to school. He's eating tall green grass.

"Does the grass taste good?" asks Bear. "I've never eaten grass. I've eaten acorns, berries, and even bugs!"

"I eat those too," says Bird. "And sometimes worms."

Fawn is surprised. "Is it strange to eat grass? Am I the only one?"

"It's just different," says Bear. She can see that Fawn is a little worried.

"Owl gave us a mantra," says Bird. "It's a reminder of how we may be different in some ways, but we are all also the same."

Bear and Bird take a deep breath in . . .
and let the air all the way out. They say
the mantra.

"Breathe in, breathe out.
Everybody has a heartbeat.
Breathe in, breathe out.
It's a rhythm we all share."

Fawn takes a long, deep breath in . . .
and lets it out. He says the mantra too.

"Breathe in, breathe out.
Everybody has a heartbeat.
Breathe in, breathe out.
It's a rhythm we all share."

Can you take a deep breath in
and let it out?
Can you say the mantra?

"I see!" Fawn says. "We all eat different things, but eating does the same job for all of us."

"Eating good food keeps our bodies healthy and strong!" chirps Bird.

"Different bellies need different foods," says Bear.

What do you like to eat?

The friends go down the sunshiny path together.
They're getting closer and closer to school!

Bear wonders what school will be like.

What do you wonder about?

The butterflies flutter in Bear's tummy. She takes a deep breath in . . . and lets it out. She says the mantra to herself.

"Breathe in, breathe out.
Everybody has a heartbeat.
Breathe in, breathe out.
It's a rhythm we all share."

Can you take a deep breath in and let it out? Can you say the mantra?

Bear notices that she walks, Bird flies, and Fawn skips.
"Friends don't have to do things the same way," thinks Bear.

How do you get to school?

At last, they arrive at school. Bear, Bird, and Fawn look around at all the animals. No one is quite like anyone else. Everyone is unique and special in their own way!

And look who the teacher is! "Good morning!" says Owl. "I'm sure you're excited and maybe a little anxious about meeting new friends. Let's all take a deep breath in . . . then let it out. Now repeat after me:

"Breathe in, breathe out.
Everybody has a heartbeat.
Breathe in, breathe out.
It's a rhythm we all share."

Bear smiles and puts her paws on her heart.
She feels her heartbeat, strong and good. She says
the mantra with the other students. She knows
these words!

"Breathe in, breathe out.
Everybody has a heartbeat.
Breathe in, breathe out.
It's a rhythm we all share."

The butterflies are out of her tummy and up in the sky, where they belong.
She feels ready for the school day to begin!

Can you put your hands on your heart?

Can you feel your heartbeat, strong and good?

You're ready for the day!

"Breathe in, breathe out.
Everybody has a heartbeat.
Breathe in, breathe out.
It's a rhythm we all share."

Find the FREE SONG
"Everybody's Got a Heartbeat"
at kirawilley.com/books!